BEING A BIG DEAL

42 DAY DEVOTIONAL
for Your Weight Loss Journey

BRITTANY CLAY

Being a Big Deal
Copyright © 2016 Brittany Clay

Cover Design by SW Designs Studio
Edited by Darilynn Hammond

Unless otherwise stated, Scripture is taken from, The Holy Bible, the English Standard Version® (ESV®) Copyright © 2001 by Crossway, a publishing ministry of Good News Publishers. All rights reserved. ESV Text Edition: 2011

Also used: The Holy Bible, New International Version (NIV) copyright© 1973, 1978, 1984 by International Bible Society.

Also used: New American Standard Bible® (NASB), Copyright © 1960, 1962, 1963, 1968, 1971, 1972, 1973, 1975, 1977, 1995 by The Lockman Foundation. Used by permission. (www.Lockman.org)

Also used: The Amplified® Bible, Copyright © 1954, 1958, 1962, 1964, 1965, 1987 by The Lockman Foundation. Used by permission. (www.Lockman.org)

Also used: The New Living Translation (NLT), copyright 1996, 2004. Used by permission of Tyndale House Publishers, Inc., Wheaton, Illinois 60189. All rights reserved.

Also used: New King James Version (NKJV), copyright © 1979, 1980, 1982, Thomas Nelson, Inc., Publishers.

Also used: King James Version (KJV), Cambridge, 1769.

Also used: The Message (MSG). Copyright © 1993, 1994, 1995, 1996, 2000, 2001, 2002 Used by permission of NavPress Publishing Group.

Library of Congress Catalog-in-Publication Data

Clay, Brittany
Being a Big Deal 42 Day Devotional for Your Weight Loss Journey/ Brittany Clay
p. cm.

ISBN-13: 978-0692715673
ISBN-10: 0692715673

All rights reserved. This book or any portion thereof may not be reproduced or used in any manner whatsoever without the express written permission of the publisher except for the use of brief quotations in a book review. Printed in the United States of America.

I dedicate this book to the people that have felt hopeless about their weight, appearance, and the ability to change. When you think differently you become different.

"With God all things are possible!" Matthew 19:26

Acknowledgments

To Travis Garza and your incredible trainers, especially Robin Brooks and Sarah Lindsey, I would not have developed into who I have become without the Travis Garza 42 Day Fat-Loss Challenge©. I am forever grateful.

To the November 2015 through June 2016 Fit-Fam each of you have inspired me to go harder and be better every day.

To my incredibly supportive children, no lifestyle change is ever easy even when it's beneficial. Thank you for putting up with all the ups and downs on account of me.

To my rock and my number one fan, my husband, Mr. Rob Clay, you have carried me, pushed me, liberated me, and supported me endlessly. I love you entirely, with everything!

Content

	Foreword
	Introduction
Trust the Process	18
Preparation	20
Temporary Pain	22
What's your Why	24
Who's in your Corner	26
Goals	30
The Voices	32
By Faith	36
Mind Chatter	38
Time	40
Thought Power	44
It's Not About Me	46
Dominion	48
Focus	50
Opportunities	52
Relentless	56
Deny Your Flesh	68
Permanent Change	62
Praise the Lord	64
Be Encouraged	66
Keep Moving Forward	68
Rest	70
Be Grateful	72
Media Takeover	74
Support System	76
Don't Give In	78
PUSH	80
God Will Use You	82
Forgive	84
No Regrets	88
No Pressure	90
Obstacles	94
Celebrate Even Now	96
Don't Go It Alone	98
The Struggle	100
Your Feelings	102
The Journey	106
Restoration	110
Grace and Mercy	112

Maintain Your Progress	114
Don't settle	118
Begin Again	120
	Results

Foreword

I remember as a child in 6th grade going home after school and working out in my bedroom with my Montgomery Wards' weight set.

At the time, I really didn't know why I was drawn to do this when all the other kids were outside doing normal kid stuff. I suppose being a skinny kid without a father gave me some kind of need to build my confidence by putting on muscle.

I'm now approaching my 50th birthday as I write this and it's very clear why I was drawn to workout in my bedroom as young 6th grader.

You see, God starts on you early whether you realize it or not. I was a C student and did not really fit in the system, in regards to making good grades and knowing what I wanted to be some day when I grew up. Most children start at a young age knowing or seeking something they want to be someday and this serves as the direction they will take in life.

All I knew is I wanted to work out, study nutrition, and psychology. There were adult figures in my life that told me I was wasting my time and needed to go to college to be something. I was told that my passion was not going to pay the bills. This was drilled into my head for many years.

You see, when someone is told they can't do something long enough, most people will eventually believe it.

I chose to ignore the negative world around me and pursue my passion, but was always fearful of what I had been told.

My passion started off about ME. I learned nutrition so well I went on to win 4 Mr. Oklahoma titles and competed in over 126 bodybuilding shows.

Once that was over, my calling from God--which I did not know at the time--began. I wanted to change the world of overweight people. I wanted to show people how to lose weight and transform their bodies so they could be happy again. I really thought that was all they needed to be happy.

As I started my journey, I slowly started to see the truth. God opened my eyes to see that people really didn't care so much about the weight loss, they cared about conquering their "WHY".

I slowly would hear people tell me how they overcame the fear of going out in public or going to the park with their kids. Some would say their marriages were saved and it was all because of the new life I had given them. Rarely did I hear about the number they lost on the scales and so my view of what the world needed became clear. Find their "WHY" and help them to bury it.

As I approach my 50th birthday I can look back and see all the people that God has put in my life to re-assure me that I'm doing His will.

I need that because although I have overcome several obstacles in my life, once you have been told you can't do something, its evil head will show itself to try to bring you down.

Brittany Clay emailed me about her project called *Being a Big Deal: 42 Day Devotional for Your Weight Loss Journey.* The book is about Brittany going through a program of mine called the 42-Day Fat Funeral Program or the (6-week) Challenge for short.

I read the introduction through Day 5 and that was all I needed to know this is on such a personal and deeply emotional level that Brittany could touch people's lives just by relating to them with this book.

You see, people want to be understood and want to know that there are people out there going through the same things they are. They want to know their fear is understood and know that someone out there has an answer to their fear whom they can trust. They want to know it can be overcome and victory is theirs for the taking.

We were not meant to do this thing called LIFE alone. God put us here for many reasons, but one main reason was to help each other. The older I get, the more I realize something I discovered years ago--It's NOT about me.

Brittany has realized this by writing this book that will empower, motivate, and most of all comfort you that you can overcome the words ***I can't*** and that voice in your head that says, "I'm not good enough."

My only request is this. Simply read what she is saying, but most importantly hear what she is saying.

I wish you the best and I love ya!

Travis L. Garza

C.P.F.S, D.T.

Introduction

When God makes everything turn in your favor, the proof lines up, the money comes in, and you can't live another day overweight and do nothing about it.

I have been conscious about my weight from the time I was in second grade. I vividly remember a Sunday morning, as my family was rushing to get ready for church my mother asked me to put my shoes on. I tried and tried but I couldn't. My mom was so frustrated when I told her I couldn't do it. She couldn't understand how I could put my shoes on any other day, but today it was such a big deal. Finally, my seven year old mind thought, "Show her why you are having such a hard time." Once she saw that when I would bend down and my stomach was so big it was inhibiting me to reach the small latch to push through the hole to fasten my shoe she understood and she helped me. That is the first time I remember being affected by being overweight. That was the first time I remember, me being big, was a big deal. Since then I have been teased, rejected, and all but hopeful about my weight. Even at that age, I would cry out to God asking for Him to take away my desire to eat bad food. I would ask God to help me not to be greedy. I would plead with God to give me the desire to exercise.

Being a BIG Deal

Over the years, I went up and down in weight. In high school I participated in sports and I was in the best shape of my life. In adulthood I became overweight and I gradually gained more and more weight until I found myself at my peak weight of 284 pounds.

In July 2015, my husband was invited to minister at a conference in Baltimore, MD. I couldn't help but notice I was the biggest woman in attendance of over 500 people and although I had a great time it was a painful experience. I wondered to myself, "What do they think of me?" Apparently they were conscious about their weight because there weren't any women there that were obese, except me. I knew I had to change my life and I never wanted to be in that situation again.

I was embarrassed knowing that if I lost twenty, forty, or even eighty pounds that I would still be overweight. I didn't want to start a program, another diet, or a boot camp just to slide back into my old habits after a few weeks or even a few days. I was fortunate to have no major health issues associated with my obesity, but this disqualified me from most weight loss surgeries. Honestly, I wanted a doctor to cut off or suck out all of the fat. I thought then I'd be happy and could move on but people kept saying, "You can gain it back." I knew that if there was a way to gain the weight back, I would find it. I definitely didn't want to "go under" and still possibly gain the weight back.

I wanted a quick fix but in reality, what you are able to get quickly can also be lost just as quickly. In my case, what I lose quickly I could gain back quickly. I had to change my thinking about my health and weight loss or I would gain back any weight I lost in no time. I just wanted the fat to go

Being a BIG Deal

away and continue to eat what I wanted to eat and exercise when I felt like it. I was lazy!

I couldn't have the easy way out mentality, trying fad diets, weight loss drops and pills, or even weight loss surgeries just to speed up the process when I knew I was fully capable of reaching my weight loss goals by maintaining a healthy diet and regular exercise.

I wouldn't call myself a risk taker. I like to know what I'm getting into so that I know what to expect. My personality was the exact opposite of the journey I was about to embark upon… and yes, I was wigging out!

Fast forward. It's Saturday, October 31, 2015 and it's weigh-in day. It was just three days ago, October 28th. I sat on the front row at the orientation of Travis Garza's Fat-Loss Camp© feeling intimidated by Travis Garza as he proudly announced, "I'm trying to scare off as many of you as I can because my program is not designed for those of you that already believed you can't do it." He went on to say, "If you can't get past food being just fuel for your body, you won't make it in my program." I sat in that chair thinking, *"Oh crap, I'm the person he keeps referring to."*

He mentioned being obsessed with food… Me! He mentioned parties and fun including food…Me again! He talked about making excuses about losing weight…yep, ME TOO. Those were just a few of the factors Travis spoke of that could lead to being unsuccessful in his 6-week Fat Loss Challenge.

I didn't realize how much pride kept me sitting in that chair with an "I'll show you" attitude. I thought, *"I can have food just for fuel, bring on your hard work-out, I'll do what*

Being a BIG Deal

I have to do, I'm not weak." In that moment, I didn't have the money for the commitment deposit, the money for supplements, nor did I have any money for the food required to follow the meal plan, but I signed up anyway. I didn't even own a scale prior to then, but God provided everything I needed.

This challenge was a life-changing event. Any major event brings excitement, fear, doubt, stress, over-thinking, and so many other responses to the new changes taking place. I began feeling overwhelmed, even before the day of the weigh-in. About a week before the weigh-in, all my friends that had applied for this particular challenge had been called back and accepted. I had not. The day that I was to be notified about my acceptance had already passed. I was hurt. My husband and friends kept telling me to wait, but I just knew I had been rejected.

It was at that point that I ask the Lord to become the leader of this entire process. I asked Him to help me, strengthen me, and teach me as I "Follow the D*mn Instructions (FTDI)" the Travis Garza Fat-Loss Camp© slogan. I thanked God for the opportunity to be in the program and for Travis Garza's vision. Soon after, I found peace in my heart and turned my entire weight-loss process over to God. Not long after that prayer I received a call that I was accepted to be a part of the November 2015 42 Day Fat-Loss Challenge©. It was now time to continue to trust God throughout the process, while also trusting the process itself.

So here I am about a week after this orientation, fat, in a sports bra and some shorts, taking pictures and doing videos in front of strangers acting like I don't care, but deep down I am losing it. I feel so ashamed of my body and the fact that I *need* this opportunity. I am losing it because I don't know if I can *really* complete the challenge. Deep down I know I should be here, I know this is a proven challenge with proven results. Deep down I feel like my life will never be the same. Deep down I know the enemy is mad because I'm about to have more energy to glorify God, and take up less space so that others can join me.

After nervously standing in the weigh in line, with the people whose names started with A-D, for what seemed like hours chit-chatting with the "newbies" and "vets" that would be doing the challenge this round, it's finally my turn. This will be my "official weigh-in." As the door closes behind me, I realize I am at the point of no return. I am DOING THIS CHALLENGE. My 5'7 frame weighed in at 270 pounds. This was 98 pounds more than the weight on my driver's license and 62 pounds above my heaviest pregnancy weight. Knowing I am closer to 300lbs than I am to 200lbs is painful spiritually, mentally, emotionally, and physically. My back hurts constantly because of the weight of my breasts, I can't sit on the toilet without losing circulation, and I can no longer bare my own weight when I wear high heels. Being limited in the type of shoes I wear has its own emotional toll for a woman. With all these overwhelming emotions I can't help but think, *"I have to do this for me. I am the only one that can change this."* I was tired of being a big deal for the wrong reason. It is time to be a big deal to me. I decided I don't ever want to see this number or anything higher reflecting my weight ever again. I'm taking this 42 day journey, even with Thanksgiving coming up!

Being a BIG Deal

During the 42 days, I craved the presence of the Lord. He graced me with His presence and spoke to me specifically about my feelings and my desires. The Lord gave my family a grace for this season. He reminded me of His promises through my obedience, diligence, and sacrifice. He was always with me. God made me feel so good; I had to share this experience with as many people as I could.

This devotional is the Holy Spirit personally cheering for you and guiding you through a 42 day journey to becoming healthier not only physically, but spiritually and emotionally as well. Each daily inspiration is followed by an Old Testament and a New Testament scripture, and completed with a prayer. My prayer is that you are built up and blessed as you make these daily encouragements a part of your routine on your journey to becoming a healthier you.

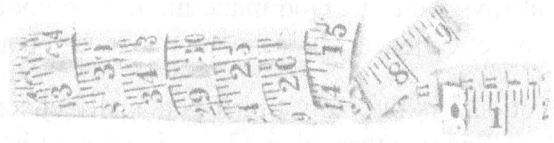

Day One

Trust the Process

Today your mind is all over the place trying to figure it all out.

"How many bags of broccoli do I need to meal prep?"
"Oh no, I don't have 5lb weights for my workout."
"What is the cost of chicken breast in bulk?"
"Do I have enough Tupperware?"
"Wait, I can drink coffee?"
"Can I really afford to do this healthy lifestyle thing?"

If you have been accepted to the Travis Garza's 6 week Fat-Loss Challenge©, you cannot afford not to do this. It has been the game changer in the lives of many. Of course there are other options, but this is the road less traveled. The results are so rewarding. Remember your "why."

If you, like many others, have an alternative plan for the next forty-two days, I applaud you for taking a step towards a healthier lifestyle.

No matter which route you take on your weight loss journey there are a few things to remember.

Being a BIG Deal

Trust is the key to the process and let me tell you, "It is a process." When you feel overwhelmed change your perspective. Begin to praise God for the opportunity, live in the present, and embrace it.

I will lead the blind by ways they have not known, along unfamiliar paths I will guide them; I will turn the darkness into light before them and make the rough places smooth. Isaiah 42:16 NIV

Do not be anxious about anything, but in every situation, by prayer and petition, with thanksgiving present your request to God. Philippians 4:6 NIV

Dear Lord,

I rejoice for you being in my life. Thank you. I know I will face obstacles but I can trust that you are with me. I do not have to worry, be anxious, or afraid. I don't know all the answers so I am asking you to be my leader and guide. Lord I will follow you so that crooked places will be made straight. I will allow your word to be a lamp unto my feet and a light unto my path. Thank you for being on this journey with me. In Jesus' name I pray. Amen.

Day Two

Preparation

In these 6 weeks you will be faced with challenges within the challenge. It is important to get prepared and stay prepared. Organize your days and set alarms. If it isn't challenging, it should not be called a challenge. This is something you've committed to, but you don't have to do it alone. You are fighting the battle of a lifetime. The internal dialogue, the emotions, and the diet change, are all reasons to focus more on God. He will make the burden of it all much lighter.

Commit your work to the Lord and your plans will be established. Proverbs 16:3

May the God of hope fill you with all joy and peace in believing, so that by the power of the Holy Spirit you may abound in hope. Romans 15:13

Being a BIG Deal

Dear Lord,

Thank you for another day of progress. Even though this is the beginning, I thank you that you are changing things for my good even now. Your Word says the steps of a good man are ordered by the Lord. So I ask that you order my steps today and throughout this journey. I commit this challenge to you so that my plan will be established. I thank you that even in the chaos, I have the yoke of the Lord upon me and I will find rest. Lord I bless you for these things. In Jesus' name I pray. Amen.

Day Three

Temporary Pain for Permanent Change

Today, if not before, the soreness from the workouts really begin to kick-in. Remember everything in life is temporary. Soon, adjustments to the meals and use of supplements will develop habits--and that's when real change begins to happen. The soreness wears off and the fat begins to melt. Be proud that it takes you about thirty seconds longer to stand up out of a chair--this too is temporary. You are preparing your body for permanent change. You are becoming a fat killing machine. YOU'VE GOT THIS!

If you faint in the day of adversity, your strength is small. Proverb 24:10

Do all things without grumbling or disputing. Philippians 2:14 NASB

Being a BIG Deal

Dear Lord,

I thank you for this day. I thank you for strengthening and sustaining me. I am glad that you Lord are my source of strength, in my mind and my body, and you continue to build me up so that in any challenge, I do not faint and I have all the strength required to overcome. I ask that you remind me of all that I have to be grateful for so that I can express my gratitude and not grumble or dispute. I know that you make all things work together for my good. In Jesus' name I pray. Amen.

Day Four

What's Your WHY?

It is important not to focus only on the weight loss. If the scale drops significantly, if it stays the same--or even if it goes up--do not let it be a distraction, especially these first few weeks. There is a number you have in mind--a goal weight--as you should. You will get there, but remember it takes time. You cannot gain twenty pounds in 2-3 days. You will not lose twenty pounds in 2-3 days. There is a reason you decided to begin this journey. That reason is your, *why*. I had many whys:

-No longer being depressed about the way my body looks
-Needing to take responsibility for what I have the power to change
-Wanting to be a role model for my children
-Never wanting to be the biggest person in a room again

Your *why* is a constant reminder that you need to make changes. God wants you to know that He knows your every why. When you feel like your *why* is becoming

Being a BIG Deal

burdensome, He wants you to talk to Him about it. God doesn't want your *why* to be the cause for depression, hopelessness, fear, or retreat. God wants your *why* to be motivating, and inspiring to you. Tell Him about your *why*. When subtle lies try to trigger negative emotions, remember, "He makes all things work together for your good."

"'For I know the plans I have for you,' declares the Lord, 'plans for welfare and not for evil, to give you a future and a hope.'" Jeremiah 29:11

But let patience have her perfect work, that ye may be perfect and entire, wanting nothing. James 1:4 KJV

Dear Lord,

Thank you for having a plan already established for me. I turn all my plans for my own life over to you Lord so that you can fine tune them to fit your master plan for your glorification. I thank you Lord for giving me a "why". It will continuously remind me of where I am, where I was, and where I am headed. I ask that you keep the negative thoughts that try to disrupt the progress I am making at bay. I will trust in knowing that you are making all things work together for my good. In Jesus' name I pray. Amen.

Day Five

Who's in Your Corner?

With any kind of change you will have the supporters, the encouragers, the doubters, the critics, the skeptics, the so-called advisors, and the haters. Jesus also encountered all these type of people when he walked the Earth.

Before Jesus was crucified, He was denied by Peter, a close friend and disciple of His. Prior to that, Jesus was betrayed by Judas--another friend and disciple of His. The one thing that stands out in both of these stories is that Jesus knew that He would be denied and by whom. Jesus also knew that He would be betrayed and by whom. Both Peter and Judas were part of Jesus' close circle.

You may not be denied or betrayed during this challenge, but you will experience interesting mindsets and conversations in regard to the challenge. People that are genuinely interested in your well-being--and some that have selfish motives--may be the same folks you catch

Being a BIG Deal

criticizing you for sticking to the meal plan, or suggesting other options, or offering you their opinion and advice. You may even have to take the criticism from close family and friends.

Thank God for the Fit-Fam--those going through and those that have successfully completed this process that keep you accountable and encouraged. Reaching out and staying connected to the group is an important and valuable resource on your journey to success. Having a support system that can relate to your struggles and victories is critical during this journey.

You are not alone and you should stay prepared for anything that might try to stand in your way of following the instructions! At this point, the challenge is in full effect. Stick to your decision to become a better you so that you can serve God in an even greater capacity.

No weapon that is formed against thee shall prosper; and every tongue that shall rise against thee in judgment thou shall condemn. This is the heritage of the servants of the Lord, and their righteousness is of me, says the Lord. Isaiah 54:17 KJV

But He turned and said to Peter, "Get behind Me, Satan!" You are a stumbling block to me; for you are not setting your mind on God's interests, but man's. Matthew 16:23 NASB

Being a BIG Deal

Dear Lord,

Thank you for sending your Son, Jesus. He set so many great examples, all while having every intention to save me. I thank you for leading me not into temptation, but delivering me from all evil. I know that all people do not intend to get me off track or to be offensive with their opinions, observations, and suggestions, so Lord have mercy on me. Give me grace to extend to all those that may knowingly or unknowingly lead me toward not following the plans you have placed before me. Thank you for answering my prayer. In Jesus' name I pray. Amen

Day Six

Goals

Where are you headed? What can you look at every day that gives you a glimpse of your envisioned fitness goals? It is so important to visualize your destination before and during your journey. Before I take a trip, I go to Google Maps and determine a route from my home to my desired location. Sometimes the map will show detours, delays, inclement weather, and whether or not the route is clear.

In life, however, when we set out to do something great, especially something different and new, we are not able to determine when, where, or what delays and detours will come up. We can, however, identify our point A and our point B. In this case, point A is your current weight, body image, and strength. Point B is your desired weight or body image, and strength. Point B is your goal. Having goals set to help reach your dreams is imperative.

Being a BIG Deal

The Word tells us, "Where there is no vision, the people perish." Continue to seek God's guidance in setting goals and trust Him to equip you to accomplish each one.

Delight yourself in the Lord, and he will give you the desires of your heart. Psalm 37:4 NASB

Now finish the work, so that your eager willingness to so it may be matched by your completion of it, according to your means. 2 Corinthians 8:11 NIV

Dear Lord,

It is you that has given me the desires I have to improve. I pray that with instruction from your Word and your grace to be obedient I will fulfill each goal. I pray that I finish well and that you receive all the glory in all that I do. Thank you for your help. In Jesus' name I pray. Amen.

Day Seven

The Voices

Everything about being healthier starts with the voices. There are two voices. The voice you follow will always be the strongest voice in your life.

Voice ONE is precise, never forceful, and you can feel the security in the words spoken to you. It always feels right. It is not easy to follow Voice ONE when you have been disobedient or simply ignoring it. Voice ONE can be heard louder and clearer the more you listen and obey the instructions spoken to you. Voice ONE is the voice of Holy Spirit who is our true comforter and guide. The Holy Spirit is gentle, consistent, and patience. The Holy Spirit is not aggressive, does not impose, and will not force the instructions. It is completely up to you to decide which voice to follow.

Being a BIG Deal

Voice TWO is discouraging, yet tempting and pleasurable, saying things like, "Go ahead and splurge, you deserve it." In the back of your mind, you know the difference between deserving and needing. You know when you do not NEED to splurge. This voice is the voice of self-gratification, selfishness, and destruction. Voice TWO is The Enemy. Voice TWO will attempt to entice you with false comforts and things that supply limited satisfaction so that it would seem like Voice ONE and the instructions of Voice ONE are unnecessary. Like Voice ONE, Voice TWO can be heard more clearly when you give in to the instructions it has spoken to you. Voice TWO can be diminished when you listen to and obey the words of Voice ONE.

God has instructed, equipped, and strengthened you to obey His Word. It will make your life much smoother to know you are operating according to what the Lord has specifically spoken to you. Its starts with saying yes to your spirit urging you to change. When you begin to give in to that little voice you allow it to take over more and more.

This day I call the heavens and earth as witnesses against you that I have set before you life and death, blessings and curses, Now choose life so that your children may live and you may love the Lord your God, listen to his voice, and hold fast to him. For the Lord is your life, and he will give you many years in the land he swore to give to your fathers, Abraham, Isaac, and Jacob. Deuteronomy 30:19-20 NIV

Whoever sows to please their flesh, from the flesh will reap destruction; whoever sows to please the Spirit, from the Spirit will reap eternal life. Galatians 6:8 NIV

Being a BIG Deal

Dear Lord,

Thank you for being so loving and patient with me. Thank you God for being faithful to me even in times that I have ignored and disobeyed your voice. Father, forgive me. I pray for fine tuning to Your Voice when you are speaking. I pray for increased obedience to follow through on all the instructions coming directly to me from God Almighty. Lord I will pray that I no longer take for granted that I can have dialogue with you. I choose to listen and obey this day. In Jesus' name I pray. Amen.

Day Eight

By Faith

In virtually every area of life, you can develop different ways to achieve similar results. That is fine. However, when you decide to go with a program that already has a system in place you should do what the system entails. Some things are set in place for your protection and to produce specific results. Going through all the explanations of why you are asked to do this or that can take up too much time and still wouldn't allow you to fully comprehend the purpose. It is important to respect the guidance that has been given and trust the basic information.

God requires us to have faith. The Word specifically says that without faith it is impossible to please God. Place your life in God's hands and allow him to carry you through. Make your decisions with discernment so that you stay in a position that pleases God. Trusting man is not required. Trusting God through man-made ideas and systems is not only required but preferred.

Being a BIG Deal

It is better to take refuge in the Lord than to trust in man. Psalm 118:8 NASB

And without faith it is impossible to please him, for whoever would draw near to God must believe that he exists and that he rewards those who seek him. Hebrews 11:6

Dear Lord,

Thank you for guidance and ensuring that I don't have to figure all things out on my own. Lord you have given me people, things, and ideas, to help improve the quality of my life. Lord I ask that my life is not consumed with these things but consumed with you so that these things are beneficial and not overwhelming to me. Help me with my faith that I may please you God. In Jesus' name I pray. Amen.

Day Nine

Mind Chatter

Being healthy is never just about how much you weigh. Health is a conglomeration of things that includes your mental state, physical state, emotional state, spiritual state, and even your relationships. All of these areas in life are instrumental to your overall health. When your spirit is healthy you are able to allow the Lord to regulate your mind--which is the driving component to how you respond internally and externally to all things.

It is your mind that moves you through different emotions and affects how you feel. It is your mind that that allows you to determine if you will or won't complete a task and then your body responds. When you are ready for change you must change your mind. The Word tells us, "For as he thinks in his heart, so is he." It will be your mind that will catapult you to the next level of any area in your life. Begin

Being a BIG Deal

to believe in yourself. Begin to think as though your goals have already been reached and everything else will respond accordingly.

You keep him in perfect peace whose mind is stayed on you because he trusts in you. Isaiah 26:3

To put off your old self, which belongs to your former manner of life and is corrupt through deceitful desires, and to be renewed in the spirit of your minds, and to put on the new self, created after the likeness of God in true righteousness and holiness. Ephesians 4:22-24

Dear Lord,

You are an incredible God. You do amazing things in amazing ways. You have given us all things that pertain to life and godliness. I am astounded at the privilege of power you have given me through my mind. I want my mind to reflect what you have called me to do and glorify and honor you. I commit my mind and my thoughts to you and I ask that you regulate them. I honor you for the peace you have given to me. In Jesus' name I pray. Amen.

Day Ten

Time

When aspiring to reach goals, everything doesn't adjust to what you are trying to accomplish. There are still twenty four hours in a day, bills continue to come, and there will still be a variety of things that occur out of your control. Addressing scheduling issues and growing more creative in how you manage time spent with loved ones is all part of the process. In a new venture, you must consider being intentional with your time. When you are blessed to implement anything new in your life, no matter how much time it demands, it is important to look at the things that already exist in your life. To your advantage, make yourself aware of the activities that may expire, the routines that will be tweaked, and the commitments that will be maintained. Below are four ways to ensure you are being intentional with your time:

Being a BIG Deal

Pray

Pray that God orders your steps and directs your path each and every day. Don't forget He is always with you and it is your responsibility to take advantage of that amazing privilege, trusting that the Lord will never lead you into destruction.

Have a calendar and schedule your day

When you allot time for the things that are mandatory and the things that are important to you, you will gain a sense of balance. Implementing a calendar allows you to control your time versus others dictating how your life will be spent.

Maintaining a calendar allows you to be productive and can be used as a tool to keep you from over-extending yourself and feeling guilty about neglecting certain things that are important to you.

Eliminate time thieves

A time thief is anything that you do that doesn't allow you to be productive toward your goals. To determine your time thieves you must be honest with yourself. Things like social media (Facebook, Twitter etc.), watching TV, playing games (Candy Crush Angry Birds etc.), talking on the phone, spending time in unnecessary places, surfing the net, are all examples of time thieves. Your time thieves can be the same as other people you know or they can be different. Examine your own life and get rid of all the things stealing your time.

Being a BIG Deal

Take Action
When God tells you to do something there is nothing to debate. It is time for you to take action. Even when you do not know what the outcome will be you must trust him. Faith without works is dead and without faith it is impossible to please Him. Have faith and do the work.

So teach us to number our days that we may get a heart of wisdom. Psalm 90:12

Look carefully then how you walk, not as unwise but as wise, making the best use of the time, because the days are evil. Therefore do not be foolish, but understand what the will of the Lord is. Ephesians 5:15-17

Dear Lord,

You are so gracious Lord. You have given me a choice in every area of my life. Lord I want to choose to be a good steward of my time. Help me to implement the beneficial things. Help me not to neglect the important things. My desire is to live by faith--pleasing you and fulfilling my purpose. I know with you God that is possible. In Jesus' name I pray. Amen.

Day Eleven

Thought Power

Your mind is very powerful. It can dictate the way you feel and it can tell you that you will succeed, or that you will not succeed. I have had thoughts come to my mind telling me to give up during a workout and not even a second later a thought reminding me I was fully capable of completing the workout. The definition of a thought is: *an idea or opinion produced by thinking occurring suddenly in the mind.* Knowing that a thought is just an idea or opinion gives you total power. It means that you have a choice. You can believe whatever thought you want to believe. We are instructed in God's Word to *cast down every imagination that exalts itself against the knowledge of God, and take every thought captive to obey Christ.* Don't ever give in to lying thoughts. If the thought goes against what the Bible says, it is a lie. Remember, with God all things are possible.

Trust in the Lord with all your heart, and do not lean on your own understanding. Proverbs 3:5

Being a BIG Deal

We destroy arguments and every lofty opinion raised against the knowledge of God, and take every thought captive to obey Christ. 2 Corinthians 10:5

Dear Lord,

Thank you for giving me such a complex mind. You have created me in your image and you are Creator. Anything that I can think of can be, so I need you Lord to help me take my thoughts captive to obey Christ. I want to live in the way you have designed and I know it all starts with how I think. Lord I trust you and I want my thoughts to align with you and your will. I thank you Lord for aligning my thoughts. In Jesus' name I pray. Amen.

Day Twelve

It's Not About Me

Once I committed to improving my health-- by working out and eating better--I noticed I had supporters. People that were rooting me on because they were inspired or because they genuinely cared about me becoming healthier. I began to receive questions about the program I was in, about the workouts, and about what I was eating. Just because I had results people began to believe in themselves. I became influential. I became the light that shone in the darkness and encouraged people to move beyond their contentment with their own uncomfortable situations. I gained followers on social media. I gained a family through the challenge. I became an illustration of hope to the hopeless.

People that had been stagnant decided to join a movement to lose weight because I was consistent. If I had given up, I would have satisfied the doubters, let myself down, and inspired no one. This certainly is not about what I have done but about how God can use me even in a situation I

Being a BIG Deal

know nothing about. He can use you too. Even when you want to give up, God is purposefully leading you to into His glorious work. You are an inspiration and someone needs you to finish so that they can begin.

So you will find favor and good success in the sight of God and man. Proverbs 3:4

You are the light of the world. A city set on a hill cannot be hidden. Nor do people light a lamp and put it under a basket, but on a stand, and it gives light to all in the house. In the same way, let your light shine before others, so that they may see your good works and give glory to your Father who is in heaven. Matthew 5:14-16

Dear Lord,

Thank you for using even me to lift you up during times that I didn't even know I could be used to glorify you. I do not take this lightly and I am honored to be a light that shines so that you Lord can be seen in me through any situation. I give you praise and honor. In Jesus' name I pray. Amen.

Day Thirteen

Dominion

It is absolutely a desire of the Lord for His children to be healthy. The Bible says that your body is the temple of God because the Holy Spirit dwells in you. When I think about the temple of God, I consider a beautiful, reverenced place. It is peaceful, comforting, and available for all to worship God. In the natural sense, we don't look at our bodies in this fashion, but we should. God created you in His image and you should have a desire to maintain His image and optimal health for your body. God's design for you to have dominion in the Earth is difficult to fulfill in an unhealthy body. You must be healthy to have dominion.

Then God said, 'Let us make man in our image, after our likeness. And let them have dominion over the fish of the sea and over the birds of the heavens and over the livestock and over all the earth and over every creeping thing that creeps on the earth.' Genesis 1:26

Being a BIG Deal

And we all, with unveiled face, beholding the glory of the Lord, are being transformed into the same image from one degree of glory to another. For this comes from the Lord who is the Spirit. Colossians 3:18

Dear Lord,

It is very humbling that you have given me dominion in the Earth. My desire is to live my life according to how you have designed it. Thank you for your grace that is allowing me to strip off my pride and trust you more. I put my life into your hands now and ask that you help me continue to become as fit and as healthy as I can be so that I can fulfill the destiny you have designed for me. In Jesus' name I pray. Amen.

Day Fourteen

Focus

Reaching goals is all about what you believe and what you focus on. Belief opens the door for possibility. It makes way for mind blowing experiences. Belief gives you the courage to persevere and work hard to reach your goals.

Focus is what keeps you on track; it keeps the vision clear so that you will not be easily deterred from your goal.

You will find joy knowing that when you focus on the Lord as He helps you reach your goals you can do anything. A promise to you is, "With God all things are possible!" Let God be your focus and you will have the goals, dreams, and abundant life you desire.

Let your eyes look directly forward, and your gaze be straight before you. Proverb 4:25

Being a BIG Deal

But seek first the kingdom of God and his righteousness, and all these things will be added to you. Matthew 6:33

Dear Lord,

I know I sometimes get distracted with trouble and worry, please forgive me. Lord I will focus on you and the directions of your voice. I know by focusing on you and the things of you distractions and all ungodliness will not be able to take hold of my life and sway it in any direction away from you. I now place all my goals in your hands. I know when I doubt, it blocks the road to my goals but when I believe, it makes my goals more reachable and attainable. Lord my prayer is to be closer to you, to seek you in every area of my life and not just when I'm in trouble. I know Lord that you are always with me and you will help me reach my goals. For that I thank you and praise you. In Jesus' name I pray. Amen.

Day Fifteen

Opportunities

One of my favorite stories in the Bible is when Peter walked on the water. This story is all about opportunity. The disciples immediately felt fear and doubt when they saw Jesus walking on the water. I know when I am not sure about what exactly God is doing I tend to want the Lord to reveal Himself or His plans to me. Then I can prepare to respond versus having faith that God is with me and will not fail me. How I would normally respond when God commands me to do something I may not be familiar with is how Peter responded, pleading with the Lord, "If it's you God, let me walk on the water and come to you."
Jesus said, "Come." He allowed Peter to walk on the water.

God gives you opportunities to walk on water all the time by using your faith to trust Him. When you ask God to perform a miracle and allow you to do great things and God says yes, how do you handle opposition that is headed your

Being a BIG Deal

way? Do you begin to focus on the opposition and challenges or do you instead focus on God?

When Peter stepped out of the boat he knew there was no bridge, or smaller boat to help him on his trek to meet Jesus. He stepped in the water out of excitement, not in faith. He was obedient, but not focused. Peter began to look around and notice the winds and the storm and became afraid. Peter was afraid to continue doing the one thing Jesus told Him to do, "Come," and Peter began to sink. When Peter began to sink, he cried out, "Lord save me!" Immediately, Jesus stretched his hand out and caught Peter and saved him.

Think about that last sentence. Jesus stretched his hand out and caught him. So if Jesus was close enough to stretch out his hand and catch Peter that means Peter wasn't that far from his destination. He was closer to his destination than he probably realized. This is why it is so important to stay focused on the thing you have set out to do.

When you are given the opportunity to do something you should always seek God to see if it is something He wants you to do. If you know God has called you to do something, you must be obedient and focus on Him while operating in that call. Every good opportunity is not a God opportunity. Even when you find yourself in a situation where you have lost focus on God and you seem to be sinking remember no matter how far away you feel like you are from Jesus, when you cry out he will come to your rescue immediately. God is always with you.

Being a BIG Deal

Yea, though I walk through the valley of the shadow of death, I will fear no evil: for thou art with me; thy rod and thy staff shall comfort me. Thou shalt prepare a table before me in the presence of my enemies; thou hast anointed my head with oil; my cup is running over. Surely goodness and mercy shall follow me all the days of my life: and I will rest in the house of the LORD forever. Psalm 23

And immediately Jesus stretched forth his hand, and caught him, and said unto him, O thou of little faith, wherefore didst thou doubt? Matthew 14:24-31 KJV

Dear Lord,

God you are so incredible. Thank you for having faith in me and trusting me even when I struggle to trust myself and you. You are a good and gracious God that will never leave me or forsake me. Thank you. Help me stay focused and obedient to the things you want me to accomplish in life. Holy Spirit, remind me to consult with you about my every decision so that it can begin blessed and I do not waste time doing something that is unfruitful. Lord I thank you that you did not give me a spirit of fear but of power, love, and a sound mind. In Jesus' name I pray. Amen

Day Sixteen

Relentless

Keep going. Don't quit. Try harder. Do it again.

On more days than not, you will experience many unexpected scenarios. You will encounter conditions contrary to that of which you desire. For example, you may fall ill, get a flat tire, or be expected to handle an abrupt change of plans.

Keep going. Don't quit. Try harder. Do it again.

There will be challenges that make you question if you can finish what you have started. You will have cravings, you will get tired, you will be questioned consistently about why you have to do certain things a certain way.

Keep going. Don't quit. Try harder. Do it again.

You will want to stop. *Keep going.* You will think about quitting. *Don't quit.* You will be uncomfortable. *Try harder.* You will be successful. *Do it again.*

Only you can take the necessary action steps to live your dreams!

Keep going. Don't quit. Try harder. Do it again.

Being a BIG Deal

Even in darkness light dawns for the upright, for the gracious and compassionate and righteous… He will have no fear of bad news; his heart is steadfast, trusting in the Lord. Psalm 112:4, 7 NIV

But our way is not that of those who shrink back to destruction, but [we are] of those who believe [relying on God through faith in Jesus Christ, the Messiah] and by this confident faith preserve the soul. Hebrews 10:39 AMP

Dear Lord,

You are so good to me. Thank you. I have witnessed you do mighty works on my behalf. When worry tries to fatigue me, you save me. When I let troubles overwhelm me, you pull me out. You are always here for me. I know that if I delight myself in You, You will give me the desires of my heart. Thank you for being so faithful, gracious, and generous to me. Thank you for seeing me better than I see myself because of the sacrifice of Jesus. I give you all honor for this prayer and the fruit to come. In Jesus' name I pray. Amen.

Day Seventeen

Deny Your Flesh

It is important to habitually give in to the spirit and deny the flesh. Denying the flesh means to concentrate on producing fruits of the spirit; it means not giving in to unhealthy cravings.

When you deliberately choose to love, be kind, create peace, extend patience, show goodness, practice faithfulness, be gentle and have self-control you are both denying the flesh and building up the spirit inside of you. Giving in to unhealthy desires can have the potential to create disasters in your life. Even partially satisfying unhealthy desires can quickly become engulfing—jeopardizing your sanity, relationships, and your productivity for God.

Here's an example:

There is a dessert you would like to eat. You get the dessert and take it home. You know there are more than enough servings for you alone. You eat one piece, knowing you should not have anymore, but it tastes so good. You cannot resist, you have another, you begin to justify why you

Being a BIG Deal

should be able to eat the entire piece if you like. You begin to reason with yourself, you think out loud, "I bought it," I'm grown and can eat whatever I want," and "I'll cut back on what I eat tomorrow."

Tomorrow is now here, and you've forgotten your friend is taking you to your favorite restaurant for lunch because she has some exciting news. You are not about to pass up a free meal, especially not your favorite free meal.

When you get home, an amazing aroma hits you and takes you some place heavenly. You had forgotten about your lunch date and that you would have leftovers so you created a comfort meal in the crock pot and it's there just waiting for you to consume, so you indulge.

After realizing you are completely off track you become hard on yourself. You throw yourself a pity party that lasts another day or two; all while eating crap to suppress your feelings.

By the time you get motivated to eat better and get back in the exercise groove; you have gained a few more pounds and lost a few days. You eventually get back on track but you wonder how you ever got so far off in the first place and it all leads back to giving in to your flesh.

Remember to trust the right voice. Feed the voice that is rooting for you so that it can be the loudest voice.

He that hath no rule over his own spirit is like a city that is broken down and without walls. Proverbs 25:28 KJV

For the grace of God that bringeth salvation hath appeared to all men, teaching us that, denying ungodliness and worldly lusts, we should live soberly, righteously, and godly, in this present world; Titus 2:11-14 KJV

Being a BIG Deal

Dear Lord,

You are a good God and a faithful God. You have always given me free will and choices and that is why it is so important that I put all my faith, trust, and hope in you. I know that in my own strength I will fail, but with the Lord I cannot fail. You will always have a safety net to catch me when I make mistakes. I am so thankful for that. Lord, teach me and help me to have self-control so that I may see results in my life that only come from disciplined action. I will give you all the credit Lord. In Jesus' name I pray. Amen.

Day Eighteen

Permanent Change

When rules and regulations are in place, it is human nature to find the easy way out. We are pleasure seekers. We tend to avoid the thing in life that seems the least pleasurable. Even necessary things such as work, dealing with debt, relationship issues, and weight loss can get neglected until there is an urgent need to fix the problem. Generally, at this point we look for a quick fix. Maybe at some point when you knew your weight was headed out of control you tried a quick fix-- a fad diet, a tea, a wrap, or a pill. You soon realized, this may work temporarily but for lasting results you must make lasting changes.

I have found that my greatest changes have formed in the presence of God. Allow your attention to remain on Him as He leads you, shows you that it is in Him that we live, and move, and have our being. He will mold you into who He has designed you to become. He will sculpt you into a new being-- chipping away the desires of who you are and who you should be that came from worldly influences. No

Being a BIG Deal

permanent change is made in your own strength. It is only by the grace of God. We were not created to be perfect, but to trust a perfect God to perfect all thing in our lives.

The Lord is my strength and my shield; my heart trusts in him, and he helps me. My heart leaps for joy, and with my song I praise him. Psalm 28:7 NIV

God's law was given so that all people could see how sinful they were. But as people sinned more and more, God's wonderful grace became more abundant. Romans 5:20 NLT

Dear Lord,

I praise you today. You are my strength, my heart trusts in you, and you help me. I am excited to know I am being led by perfection into perfection. I thank you that your grace and mercy trumps all my mistakes and challenges. I want to remain focused on you Lord as you guide me into the life you have designed for me. I love you with all my heart and thank you. In Jesus' name I pray. Amen.

Day Nineteen

Praise the Lord

When life happens--you oversleep and miss your only option for a workout class, you come home to your protein shake mix spilled in the litter box, or it's 7:30am and you have to be at work at 8:00am and you go to grab your breakfast only to realize your roommate ate your very last bag of egg muffins and you're out of eggs--what do you do?

As crazy as this may seem, you find praise. Praising God is a game changer. When you praise God, He begins to shift your focus from your problems to your solution. In praise you find peace, hope, joy and a portal to worship. God changes the atmosphere through your praise; He has control in these moments to change your perspective and change your situation.

In the Bible, Paul and Silas were in prison for serving God. While they were in prison, a very unlikely place to find a reason to praise God, they began to sing praises. They were so loud, the other prisoners listened and all of a sudden there was an earthquake that shook the prisons so that

Being a BIG Deal

immediately all the doors were opened and their chains were broken.

When you are able to praise God through difficult times, others will witness you. Through your praises, God will not only change your situation, He will cause others to be set free because of your praise.

You have the ability to turn any day around with praises to the Lord.

This is the day that the Lord has made, let us rejoice and be glad in it. Psalm 118:24

And at midnight Paul and Silas prayed, and sang praises unto God; and the prisoners heard them. And suddenly there was a great earthquake, so that the foundations of the prison were shaken: and immediately all the doors were opened, and everyone's bands were loosed. Acts 16:25-26 KJV

Dear Lord,

I thank you for this day. I pray that you bring praise to my lips in every situation. I know that complaining will never help the situations I face so in your strength, I will be thankful always. I release your power over all my worries and problem and I will rejoice in this day because you have made it and allowed me to make the best of it. Thank you for new grace and mercy-- a clean slate with limitless possibilities. In Jesus' name I pray. Amen.

Day Twenty

Be Encouraged

This is the day that the Lord has made, rejoice and be glad in it! It is an incredible feeling to notice yourself doing those things that you may not have found yourself doing just last week. Triumph in this! God is pleased with your effort to build His Temple (your body) up. Celebrate your victories off the scale as if the challenge has been successfully completed. Every step you take closer is BIG. Celebrate it like you would if you were celebrating a close friend's accomplishments. Keep up the good work. You are AMAZING because God created you that way.

A joyful heart is good medicine, but a crushed spirit dries up the bones. Proverbs 17:22

Therefore, my beloved brothers be steadfast, immovable, always abounding in the work of the Lord, knowing that in the Lord your labor is not in vain. 1 Corinthians 15:58

Being a BIG Deal

Dear Lord,

I am so grateful to notice the changes coming that I have put effort towards. I want to have a good attitude towards my accomplishments. I know I could be where I was just a few weeks ago--doing nothing with no plan. Since that is not the case, I am grateful. Lord I will look for reminders that I am not where I was, but I am on my way to something greater. I thank you God for giving me strength to be successful every day. I love you with all my heart. In Jesus' name I pray. Amen.

Day Twenty One

Keep Moving Forward

You have been in the process of changing your lifestyle for 3 weeks. You are at the midpoint of this challenge and there is no reason to turn back now. At this point, you should notice changes in the way you look, the way your clothes fit, and how you feel. You may even notice you are able to engage more during your workouts. These small changes are huge victories. As you continue, remember to be confident that when God begins a good work in you, He will perform it until the day of Jesus Christ. No turning back, press forward, and press in!

He gives strength to the weary and increases the power of the weak. Isaiah 40:29 NIV

Being confident of this very thing, that he which hath begun a good work in you will perform it until the day of Jesus Christ. Philippians 1:6 KJV

Being a BIG Deal

Dear Lord,

Thank you for sustaining me mentally, physically, and emotionally. Thank you for giving me strength to begin and power to endure until the end. I am so grateful that you are the Lord that cares about every detail of my life. You have led me this far and I will continue to allow you to lead me in every aspect of my life. I praise for the small changes and the huge victories. In Jesus' name I pray. Amen.

Day Twenty Two

Rest

There will always be something that demands your attention. Sometimes these very things make you feel guilty about taking a break and getting some rest. Rest doesn't necessarily mean sleep, but it does mean taking your mind to a place that gives you effortless peace. **Give yourself permission to rest.**

The things you so eagerly want to address will be there when you have finished your break. If you are unable to pull away today, plan a time when you are able to pull away. You don't have to take a full blown vacation; just take a nap or a leisurely walk. Do something that allows you to be carefree. Your body needs rest to recuperate and be healthy. If you don't know how to rest or what to do, get in the presence of God in your personal prayer time.

Alone time with God is the most refreshing and rewarding experience you can have.

Being a BIG Deal

And he said, "My presence will go with you, and I will give you rest."
Exodus 33:14

Come to me, all who labor and are heavy laden, and I will give you rest. Take my yoke upon you, and learn from me, for I am gentle and lowly in heart, and you will find rest for your souls. For my yoke is easy, and my burden is light.
Matthew 11:28-30

Dear Lord,

Thank you for reminding me to rest. I will trust you with everything that pertains to me. I give you all of my worries, problems, and fears and I ask that you do what you will with them. Your word says, "It is in vain that you rise up early and go late to rest, eating the bread of the anxious toil -Psalm 127:2." Lord help me not be anxious. I will take comfort in knowing that you love me too much for me to worry about things you will handle. Thank you for handling these things for me. In Jesus' name I pray. Amen.

Day Twenty Three

Be Grateful

It is important to keep a grateful mindset. Meal plans, food prep, and workouts can become habitual. You can find yourself going through the motions. This can be good. You've developed a mindset that says, "It is what it is" and you're doing what you have to do to reach your goals. Still, this can also be bad because you can develop a self-righteous attitude and begin feeling like you are making progress through your own strength.

Every breath you take, every motion you make, every thought you have--even waking up--is a gift from God. We should see it as such and take advantage of the opportunity to praise Him and give Him glory for it. The past few weeks and the next few weeks will only be successful by the grace of God. Give honor to God from whom all blessings flow.

The one who offers thanksgiving as his sacrifice glorifies me; to one who orders his way rightly I will show the salvation of God! Psalm 50:23

Being a BIG Deal

So, whether you eat or drink, or whatever you do, do all to the glory of God. 1 Corinthians 10:31

Dear Lord,

You are important to me. I want my life, and my lifestyle to glorify you. I don't ever want to imply I am doing anything in my own strength. Thank you Lord for always allowing me to come to you and reconcile I recommit this journey to you. I ask that you carry me through to the end. Thank you for your grace, mercy, and loving-kindness towards me. In Jesus' name I pray. Amen.

Day Twenty Four

Media Takeover

As the days have passed, I have noticed that our culture is bombarded with food. There are commercials, billboards, flyers, coupons, and people posting pictures of their meals on social media. We receive invitations to go out to eat, emails about food, texts about food, lunch meetings, and dinner dates-- food is everywhere. To make matters worse, it's the unhealthy food that is being broadcasted to the masses. I was hard-pressed to find a healthy meal without having to intentionally search for it. Unfortunately, many have been brainwashed into being obsessed with food.

Food is a multi-trillion dollar industry, which explains why there is so much effort put into keeping it on your mind. The world's system is meant to cater to our flesh. The temptations that come to get you off track have already been overcome through Jesus. Even when we fall to temptation God's grace is sufficient and He will help us through any situation.

Being a BIG Deal

Fear not, for I am with you; be not dismayed, for I am your God; I will strengthen you, I will help you, I will uphold you with my righteous right hand. Isaiah 41:10

Do not be conformed to this world, but be transformed by the renewal of your mind, that by testing you may discern what is the will of God, what is good and acceptable and perfect. Romans 12:2

Dear Lord,

You covered everything when you sent your son Jesus to the cross for me. I am forever grateful for that sacrifice. I give you my mind and thank you for renewing it. I thank you that you strengthen me so that I can overcome every temptation. My prayer is to honor and glorify you in a world that rigorously tries to keep you out. I love you and bless you Lord. In Jesus' name I pray. Amen.

Day Twenty Five

Support System

Encouragement is very empowering. It inspires, strengthens, and has a lasting effect to push fellow sisters and brothers past the most challenging times.

Surrounding yourself with positive, like-minded, people that are reaching for the same goal is a driving force to success. Be inclusive; as you are inspired, inspire another. As you are encouraged, encourage someone else. It was never God's plan for us to go through anything in life alone. In Proverbs we are told, "As iron sharpens iron, so one person sharpens another." We do not ever have to become dull in the thing we are purposed and called to do. Engage with the supportive community that God has given you. You will have an incredible outlook in any process.

Therefore encourage one another and build one another up, just as you are doing. 1 Thessalonians 5:11

And let us consider how to stir up one another to love and good-works, not neglecting to meet together, as is the habit

Being a BIG Deal

of some, but encouraging one another, and all the more as you see the day drawing near.
Hebrews 10:24-25

Dear Lord,

You are so gracious to put others in my life that will help me succeed. Lord I will trust you and your Word. I will not place anything or anyone before you. I know that you are the shield for me, the glory and lifter of my head. Thank you for being the head of my support system. Lord I will open my eyes to everything and anyone you have placed in my path to encourage and support me. I know this is a blessing that you have designed just for me. Help me edify those that have supported me. Place those in my path that I may be able to help support. Give me grace to be open to the many blessings you have for me through my support system. I honor you oh Lord. In Jesus' name I pray. Amen.

Day Twenty Six

Don't Give In

There will be days when you are exposed to food that is tremendously tempting. Many of these days will be unexpected; it may be a coworker's birthday and someone brings in your favorite cupcakes to celebrate. Other days you may be more prepared--like Thanksgiving, when others persistently challenge you to get you off track. No matter how prepared you are, understand that temptation is designed to make you fail at something. A temptation is difficult to resist. The Word tells us, "No temptation has overtaken you that is not common to man. God is faithful, and he will not let you be tempted beyond your ability, but with the temptation he will also provide a way of escape, that you may be able to endure." The interesting thing about this passage is that it specifically uses the words, *escape* and *endure*.

One meaning of escape is to get away from something difficult or unpleasant. To endure means to tolerate or put up with something unpleasant.

Being a BIG Deal

In any situation you face, God has promised that you will have a way of escape and you will be able to endure, so you can rejoice and have hope in that.

Many are the afflictions of the righteous but the Lord delivers him out of them all. Psalm 34:19

No temptation has overtaken you that is not common to man. God is faithful, and he will not let you be tempted beyond your ability, but with the temptation he will also provide a way of escape, that you may be able to endure it. 1 Corinthians 10:13

Dear Lord,

You are The Most Holy One. I praise you Lord. I have left nothing to my own fate and you have made a way for my success before the beginning of time. I thank you for the Holy Spirit speaking to me in the difficult times, leading me out of temptations, and teaching me how to avoid them. God you are so good. I thank you for every promise. In Jesus' name I pray. Amen.

Day Twenty Seven

PUSH

Throughout the past few weeks, some days may have been much easier than others. It could have been easier to get out of bed, easier to workout, easier to maintain eating the right thing, and overall easier to stick with the program. When you find yourself on a wave of least-resistance take advantage. This is when you have the stamina to work hard and push yourself in areas that could use improvement. When we have an abundance of anything--such as time, energy, money, or freedom--we must optimize the potential. During these spurts of ease, when working out, take fewer breaks and focus on form for better results. When you push yourself to the best of your ability, you don't ever have to wonder "what if." You will know that the results you have are your very best. Even during the trying times, do the very best you can and the Lord will sustain you.

The soul of the sluggard craves and gets nothing, while the soul of the diligent is richly supplied. Proverb 13:4

Being a BIG Deal

Look carefully then how you walk, not as unwise but as wise, making the best use of the time, because the days are evil. Therefore do not be foolish, but understand what the will of the Lord is. Ephesians 5:15-17

Dear Lord,

You have given me so many precious gifts and I thank you for them. Help me as I go through today to make the best of my time, my energy, the liberty you have given me, and even the money I have access to. I look to you as my provision and everything that comes from you is good. I do not want to waste it. Holy Spirit, show me ways to be more effective in the areas I need to and show me how to be more grateful. In Jesus' name I pray. Amen.

Day Twenty Eight

God Will Use You

God will use you to bring him glory. You are a living testimony. What better way to show how good God is, than through the way you live your life. It's not about living perfectly; it is all about allowing others to see how God continues to have grace, mercy, favor, and blessings for you even in your imperfection. We are created to be solely dependent on the Lord.

So here's the thing, sometimes we get a glimpse of other people's lives we admire and we aspire to live like those people. Imitating people that are living a good, even wealthy, honest Christian lifestyle can offer minimal reward in comparison to what imitating God can offer. We should always aspire to live like Christ and then give God full credit for the richness you are able to experience by his grace. People will be interested, inspired, and convinced, by your weight loss experience. It is the Lord that has given you the provision and sustained you through the journey to allow you to be an inspiration. You are the

Being a BIG Deal

vessel, but Jesus is the main attraction, and it should be Him dwelling in you that others are drawn to.

I am the Lord; I have called you in righteousness; I will take you by the hand and keep you; I will give you as a covenant for the people, a light for the nations. Isaiah 42:6

Therefore be imitators of God, as beloved children. Ephesians 5:1

Dear Lord,

I am so grateful that you would use even me to be a light for you. Today I open myself to the possibilities for showing you to others in every area of my life. Thank you for allowing me to have a positive impact on others. Nothing is more positive than you and you are letting me impact others by revealing you to them. Lord you are so incredible. Thank you for everything you are doing in my life. In Jesus' name I pray. Amen.

Day Twenty Nine

Forgive

God never intended for you to figure everything out on your own. God determined soon after He created Adam that He did not want man to be alone. Man, meaning you and every other soul ever born. It is God's design that working with others generates greater potential.

In life you will be hurt by people. You have to find a way to forgive and ask God to heal you so that you can be free from the bondage that bitterness has over you when you do not forgive.

Forgiveness is a tool that helps build relationships without biases. It allows you to form relationships based on the experiences you have with an individual and not based on what you have experienced in past relationships. Forming relationships with people you can trust, leads you in the right direction for a fulfilling life. Don't just focus on forgiving others, remember to forgive yourself. There is so much more to life than working, paying bills, and dying. It is about how you live, who you inspire, and the legacy that you will leave. Building a legacy requires you to touch the

Being a BIG Deal

lives of others. Jesus set the best example of leaving a legacy.
Jesus set the best example for forgiveness.
Jesus showed us how to form relationships, especially a relationship with The Father.
Jesus--as much God as he was man and as much man as he was God--had a team, a support system. Jesus' team is still growing today.
Jesus loved!
You are no greater than Jesus, forgive and drop the weight of bitterness. Build relationships to drop the weight of loneliness and the weight of the control that you never really had. Trust God as He leads you into your destiny while maintaining peace. Love yourself and love others because love never fails.

Thou shalt not avenge, nor bear any grudge against the children of thy people, but thou shalt love thy neighbor as thyself: I am the Lord.
Leviticus 19:18 KJV

Put on then, as God's chosen ones, holy and beloved, compassionate hearts, kindness, humility, meekness, and patience, bearing with one another and, if one has a complaint against another, forgiving each other; as the Lord has forgiven you, so you also must forgive. And above all these put on love, which binds everything together in perfect harmony. Colossians 3:12-14

Being a BIG Deal

Dear Lord,

Thank you for giving me the perfect example of how to live through Christ. Lord help me forgive and show me who to forgive so that I may be free. Help me love like you so that I can live in total liberty. In Jesus' name I pray. Amen.

Day Thirty

No Regrets

Don't sit and think yourself into depression. Don't have pity-parties in your head about how you managed to get to certain points in life you are not pleased about, especially your weight. Don't sit and retrace your actions or think about the hurtful words people have spoken to you in regards to these areas in your life.

Don't blame yourself for developing relationships with people that introduced you to bad habits. Don't blame your parents for teaching you not to be wasteful, telling you to eat everything on your plate. Don't blame the media, the BMI index, and don't blame God and begin questioning Him. *Why are the most delicious foods the unhealthiest, why did he make me gain weight when my cousins can eat the same thing and stay skinny, why didn't you give me an athletic gift?*

Don't torture yourself with thoughts of things that can't be changed. God wants you to focus on Him as He changes you into who he has designed you to be. There is no time

Being a BIG Deal

for regrets when you can make the most of what you have right now.

Remember not the former things, nor consider the things of old. Behold, I am doing a new thing; now it springs forth, do you not perceive it? I will make a way in the wilderness and rivers in the desert. Isaiah 43:18-19

And after you have suffered a little while, the God of all grace, who has called you to his eternal glory in Christ, will himself restore, confirm, strengthen, and establish you. To Him be the dominion forever and ever. Amen. 1Peter 5:10-11

Dear Lord,

Thank you for giving us chance after chance to live a fulfilling life with no regrets. You tell us not to walk in condemnation and you have already forgiven us. It makes no sense to hold ourselves in contempt for things Jesus has shed His blood for and you have already forgotten. Thank you for all of these privileges. In Jesus' name I pray. Amen.

Day Thirty One

No pressure

You can be so much more critical on yourself than others are. This lack of grace is evident in the compliments you downplay or the praise from others you turn down. These actions are the product of the standards you have set for yourself. The fruit from these standards is a self-help mechanism intended to shield you from hurt, pain, and vulnerability and it is the same fruit that repels love, intimacy, and positive change. It is great to have high standards for the quality of life you desire. However, it is more important not to allow your standards, insecurities, and expectations to cloud what God has blessed you with. It is important not to take the bait of ungratefulness because you are not content with your circumstances.

Being overweight can lead to low self-esteem and feelings of unworthiness, especially if you are not careful with the standard you place upon yourself about how you look and how you have treated your body with diet and exercise.

Being a BIG Deal

Take the pressure off yourself. This doesn't mean don't take responsibility, but do not become more harsh toward yourself than God would be toward you. This pattern of living is a perfect example of Satan coming to kill, steal, and destroy. Satan wants your joy, your health, your mind, and ultimately your life. If you are consumed with pain, you are ineffective for Jesus and the calling God has on your life. Jesus said he came so that you may have life more abundantly. He always counteracts, and has already defeated, the enemy's plan for you. It is up to you to decide which plan will be active in your life. You can live in defeat or live in victory. Choose victory. Take the pressure off yourself and allow God's sufficient grace and peace to consume you.

The heart is more deceitful than all else. And is desperately sick; Who can understand it? "I, the Lord, search the heart, I test the mind, even to give to each man according to his ways, According to the results of his deeds. Jeremiah 17:9-10 NASB

For by grace you have been saved through faith; and that not of yourselves, it is the gift of God; not as a result of works so that no one may boast. For we are His workmanship, created in Christ Jesus for good works, which God prepared beforehand so that we would walk in them. Ephesians 2:8-10 NASB

Dear Lord,

I don't want the pressure you never intended for me to carry. I release it and give it to you. When I feel like I need to protect myself from being hurt, Holy Spirit, remind me that God is my protector, my shield, and that I should trust Him. Show me Lord how to love myself like you love me. Deliver me from holding on to the decisions I've made in the past that have had a negative impact in my life. You make all things work together for my good. I will not trust in my emotions, but I will trust in you Lord. In Jesus' name I pray. Amen.

Day Thirty Two

Obstacles

Weight loss is about so much more than the number on the scale. It is about determination, hard work, sacrifice, and patience regardless of what method you take to drop the pounds. There will be good days and there will be days when you want to be hard on yourself. A few reasons you may be feeling discouraged are:
- You are unsatisfied with the progress of your current weight loss
- You are dealing with how you let your weight get to where it is now
- You had a bad day with your meal plan or workout
- You don't feel supported

These, and many other factors, are all reasons that may seem warranted to be sad, angry, or defeated. The good news is, THEY ARE NOT!

The above stated reasons are all examples of obstacles. An obstacle is defined as, *a thing that blocks one's way or prevents or hinders progress*. Yes, obstacles may slow you down. Yes, obstacles may require more effort from you.

Being a BIG Deal

Obstacles however, are not a reason for you to give up. They are a reason for you to go hard. When you think your obstacle is too much to handle, that is a sign of unbelief and belief is the very thing it will take for you to overcome all the things that you feel are holding you back. With God all things are possible to them that believe. Believe!

For the vision is yet for an appointed time, but at the end it shall speak, and not lie: though it tarry, wait for it; because it will surely come, it will not tarry. Behold, his soul which is lifted up is not upright in him: but the just shall live by his faith. Habakkuk 2:3-4 KJV

Then the disciples came to Jesus in private and asked, "Why couldn't we drive it out?" He replied, "Because you have so little faith, Truly I tell you, if you have faith as small as a mustard seed you can say to the mountain, 'Move from here to there,' and it will move. Nothing will be impossible for you." Matthew 17:19-20 NIV

Dear Lord,

Help me focus on you. Lord I don't want to focus on all the things that haven't gone my way. Your Word tells me how to overcome obstacles. Guide me to those passages so that I can draw strength from what you have told us. Lord, thank you for walking with me as I reach every goal in my life. I give you glory for it God. In Jesus' name I pray. Amen.

Day Thirty Three

Celebrate Even Now

Even when you can feel the weight of responsibility lifting, the challenge does not get easier. In less than ten days you will be able to celebrate a new victory! Through the gained strength, the soreness, the cravings, and everything else that came with it, you will have completed 42 days of fitness! Over the past few weeks you have had victory, after victory. The best part is there are still more victories to follow in these last 10 days. Celebrate all the things God has made possible and shown you. Making it through a day is something to be grateful for, yet you have surpassed just making it through a day. You are taking your days and making them work for you. God is doing a new work in you. Be glad and rejoice!

See I will create new heavens and a new earth. The former things will not be remembered, nor will they come to mind. But be glad and rejoice forever in what I will create, for I will create Jerusalem to be a delight and its people a joy. Isaiah 65:17-18 NIV

Being a BIG Deal

Through him we have also obtained access by faith into this grace in which we stand, and we rejoice in hope of the glory of God. Not only that, but we rejoice in our sufferings knowing that suffering produces endurance. Romans 5:2-3

Dear Lord,

I thank you that you have allowed me to make it this far in the 42 day process. I am so thankful for all the changes I see, and even the changes that that are to come. You are a good God. You keep sustaining me so that I can give glory to you in my actions and build my body so that it is reflective of the holy temple you designed it to be. God, my heart and my mouth will be full of your praises today. I will rejoice in you always. In Jesus' name I pray. Amen.

Day Thirty Four

Don't Go It Alone

In the very first book of the Bible, God decided it was not good for man to be alone. It is a vital part of your success to seek others for counsel, guidance, and accountability. It is also important to have those in your life that you are leading and teaching. Pride keeps you in a state of being alone, believing you can achieve great things own your own. Pride also comes before fall. You must involve other people in your life to be your checkpoints and references.

God has given you instructions to be inclusive. You do not have to have a large group of people you consult--Jesus only had twelve. You will benefit greatly becoming more involved in a community working towards your goal. This can afford you the opportunity to minister where that platform may not have been available to you before. Be open, resist pride, and be lead of the Lord.

Without counsel plans fail, but with many advisers they succeed. Proverbs 15:22

Being a BIG Deal

But He gives more grace. Therefore He says: "God resists the proud, But gives grace to the humble." James 4:6 NKJV

Dear Lord,

I do not want my plans to fail. I want this journey to give me the opportunity to give out as much as I take in so that I can continue to be filled up. Show me how to continually walk in humility and yet be successful in my deeds. I will allow myself to be open to you God, I will resist pride, and let you lead. In Jesus' name I pray. Amen.

Day Thirty Five

The Struggle

It is important to keep in mind that others will never understand the way you struggle. Encountering people that discourage you --by offering their critical opinion or unhealthy food they know you aren't eating--can be frustrating. Others will never understand how certain things can trigger breakdown or why other things inspire strength. Your individual walk in life is exactly that, yours. You must seize every opportunity to live at your greatest capacity. You must thrive in any situation. You must maximize your potential. No one can thrive for you. No one else can seize an opportunity that has been granted to you. No one else can maximize your potential. Everyday lends you a new opportunity to give in to criticism and temptation and the same opportunity to yield to restraint and stay positive.

Outside voices, including your very own thoughts will drown out the voice of God. Be deliberate in recognizing God's voice. Even those you believe have close relationships with God cannot give you or tell you what can only be received directly by you from God. God may be

Being a BIG Deal

speaking to you now but you are not able to hear what HE is saying because you are not ready and clouded with other voices. Get ready to hear God. Read His Word and listen to His voice and you will be properly guided into your greatest destiny.

Then God came and stood before him exactly as before, calling out, "Samuel! Samuel!" Samuel answered, "Speak. I'm your servant, ready to listen." 1 Samuel 3:10 MSG

Beware of dogs, beware of evil workers, beware of the false circumcision; for we are the true circumcision, who worship in the Spirit of God, and glory in Christ Jesus, and put no confidence in the flesh. Philippians 3:2-3 NASB

Dear Lord,

I desire to know your voice. I want to answer your call and obey your whispers. Teach me your ways Lord. I pray for discernment to recognize your voice from the voice of the deceiver. I know you can speak through any entity and in any situation. Show me how to position myself to hear you in my life. Silence the other voices when you are speaking. I give you my mind and my heart. Thank you for giving me the victory in every struggle. In Jesus' name I pray. Amen.

Day Thirty Six

Your Feelings

In times when you feel alone, remember God has promised that He is always with you. When you feel off course or mislead, remember the Lord is constantly guiding you with His Voice, with His hand, and with His Word.

When you feel like you're not making any progress, remember the Lord has already given you the victory. It is important not to get caught up in how you feel because how you feel is only temporary. Sadness, happiness, anger, fears, disgust, and trust all waiver depending on the circumstance. You should not focus on your feelings but the vision that has been set before you. Remember what your goal is and why you set it.

A true goal will not waiver because it is measureable. For example, a goal to "be healthier" is not a goal at all. There is no way to measure this. The actual goal could be," I will spend at least a solid hour exercising 4 days a week." With this goal, you will know if you have reached it or if you have failed based on the amount of time that is actually spent exercising.

Being a BIG Deal

It is so important to write your vision so that you can remember the reason you are making the efforts to accomplish the goals.

It is important to have the facts because the facts outlast emotions. If studies show that it is a fact that it takes 500 jumping jacks to burn the calories from a candy bar, that should inspire you not to eat the candy bar.

The most important thing is being available to hear the Holy Spirit as He leads you through difficult times, buffering the rough places of the journey. This means if you have noticed your cravings increase after you exercise, you should speak with a professional--such as a nutritionist--and listen to the Holy Spirit for guidance about how to manage these cravings in order to decrease them. Both the Holy Spirit and the professional will give you insight on how to tweak what you are doing to accomplish your goals and still get maximum results.

Yet I am always with you; you hold me by my right hand. You guide me with your counsel, and afterward you will take me into glory. Psalm 73:23-24 NIV

Brothers, I do not consider that I have made it on my own, But one I do: forgetting what lies ahead, I press on toward the goal for the prize of the upward call of God in Christ Jesus. Philippians 3:13-14 ESV

Dear Lord,
I don't want to be controlled by my emotions. Lead me to accomplish my plans and dreams. I will trust you and the way you lead me. I am ready to reap so I will not become weary and I will not faint. I will get my strength from you Lord. I will remember that you are always with me, to hold

my hand, and you guide me into glory. Thank you Lord for letting me win with you. In Jesus' name I pray, Amen.

Day Thirty Seven

The Journey

The word journey means to travel from one place to another. Travel does not necessarily mean changing locations but instead, means changing the condition one is in at a specific time. You should be on a continuous journey to becoming a better person. Being successful in your health, finances, relationships and any other area can be likened to being at the peak of a mountain. Generally, no one just gets dropped off on a mountain top. If you started at the top, you were most likely born at the top. If you made it to the top after birth, you were either carried by someone or you, like most successful people, had to climb up the mountain to get there. Each individual's journey is different. People succeed for different reasons. People fail for different reasons.

There are many factors that can play into why one's journey is successful and other factors that contribute to one failing on a journey. Take a look at some factors that will likely contribute to a failing journey and some factors that can contribute to your successful journey.

Being a BIG Deal

Factors of a failing journey:
You do not have the proper equipment.
You don't know you can go to the top of the mountain.
You are too lazy to climb to the top of the mountain.
You are afraid to climb to the top of the mountain.
You have gotten too tired to continue climbing.
You have other people discouraging you from climbing to the top.
You are carrying too much to make it to the top of the mountain.

Factors of a successful journey:
You have become familiar with what it takes to get to the top of the mountain.
You have a mentor that is at the top of the mountain and can insight for your climb.
You have the proper equipment to make the climb.
You have committed to working extremely hard.
You have faith you can make the climb.
You never give up and never settle.
You surround yourself with like-minded individuals working to get to the top.
You release everything, every person, and every thought that tries to keep you from getting to the top.

Wherever you may be on your journey, consistency will keep you going in the direction you are moving toward. No matter how long you have traveled in one direction you can turn around and move toward a different path. On your journey do all that it takes to get where you would like to be located.

Being a BIG Deal

*And the L*ORD *went before them by day in a pillar of cloud to lead them along the way, and by night in a pillar of fire to give them light, that they might travel by day and by night. Exodus 13:21*

Wherefore seeing we also are compassed about with so great a cloud of witnesses, let us lay aside every weight, and the sin which doth so easily beset us, and let us run with patience the race that is set before us. Hebrews 12:1 KJV

Dear Lord,

I know that there is no journey that can compare to the journey of Christ coming from heaven to Earth, being beaten and murdered, to shed his blood and rise again for me to be saved. I will let that be my inspiration for all things in life and continue to be more like you on my journey. In Jesus' name I pray. Amen
.

Day Thirty Eight

Restoration

Expect to experience great moments on your journey and some moments that aren't so great. Remember, if you are not being productive in an area it will wither away. In the areas that you thrive in, you must eliminate the deadweight in order to continue to thrive--the things you have outgrown, and the things that have outgrown you. During these times of cutting away, it may seem hard, painful, and unnecessary, but in order for you to produce at your best it is mandatory. Sometimes it is hard to accept that it's time for people to exit your life. God has allowed for those people's purpose in your life to be served. He will give you peace and fill any void well above anything you could imagine, especially if you let go of the people and things that have been removed and hold on to Him instead.

Sometimes we have a mindset that says, "I don't know how I will make it without _____". That is the very mindset that removes God from being ruler in that area of your life and replaces Him with all the other things you are trusting in. A statement like, "I don't know how I would make it

without my job," replaces God with your job. You can fill in the blank with many things, but anything in that blank outside of God is improper. God wants you to put all your trust in Him.
God is the one that gives and the one who takes away.
If you are in a position that seems like you are losing things you cherish, do not dwell on the things you have lost. Begin to dwell in the presence of the Lord, the only place you can be fully restored.

For everything there is a season, and a time for every matter under heaven Ecclesiastes 3:1

Every branch in me that does not bear fruit He takes away, and every branch that does bear fruit He prunes, that it may bear more fruit.
John 15:2

Dear Lord,

Thank you for loving me enough to let me grow. Lord, give me strength when I have hard losses in my cutting away seasons. I know that your plan is bigger than one person's influence in my life, or the false sense of security I have in worldly things. Lord continue to lead me into your presence so that I may be whole, wanting nothing. In Jesus' name I pray. Amen

Day Thirty Nine

Grace and Mercy

This is a fight worth fighting. The pain goes away. The stress decreases. The anxiety fades. The momentum builds. You find a flow. You get stronger. You push. You don't give up.

It is up to you to choose daily how to live, how to respond, and how to perceive things.

God gives you and everyone new mercies every day.

Mercy is God blocking and withholding the consequences you deserve. Grace is God extending a blessing you do not deserve. God decides to extend His loving-kindness and grace to you even with your disbelief, disloyalty, lies, broken promises, non-praying, bitterness, and any other sin you may harbor intact. God gives you a clean slate EVERY DAY! Who are you to reject what God has done for you, to live in self condemnation and self-pity? There is nothing you can do to get rid of the grace and mercy the Lord has extended to you. You may as well live redeemed and start fresh because God Almighty has made this possible just for you.

Being a BIG Deal

It is of the Lord's mercies that we are not consumed, because His compassions fail not. They are new every morning: great is thy faithfulness. Lamentations 3:22-23 KJV

For by grace you have been saved through faith. And this is not your own doing; it is the gift of God, not a result of works, so that no one may boast. Ephesians 2:8-9

Dear Lord,

I am so very grateful for your grace and mercy. God you give us chance after chance and option after option to live blessed lives that glorify you. Holy Spirit lead me into the right places and steer me toward the right decisions. Help me to be forgiving of myself and not live in the past, walking in condemnation or self-pity. Lord I know that your grace is sufficient and in my weakness your strength is made perfect. I know that I am weak but God you are strong. Today I choose to walk with you and trust in you in everything. In Jesus' name I pray. Amen.

Day Forty

Maintain Your Progress

Don't get comfortable with how far you've come and slide back into old habits. We are instructed to be transformed--not by the renewing of our diets, or the renewing of our gym membership, but by the renewing of our minds. True change begins with the way you think. There is no way around it. If you are working hard to change a thing and all you can focus on is finishing your next steps in order to go back to the usual way you do things, then your efforts have little meaning. You will end up right back in the same position you started in.

It's like people that win the lottery and are broke in just a short period of time after they have won millions or like people that go on diets and gain more weight back after the diet is over. You cannot achieve a dream with short term projects or quick fixes.

Even God knew that it takes sacrifice, pain, and a mentality shift in order to change destinies. The life, death, and resurrection of Jesus are the perfect example of transformation. Jesus, as much God as He was man, and as

Being a BIG Deal

much man as He was God, came to Earth, dealt with human issues, helped the multitudes, was tempted by Satan, was denied and betrayed by so called friends, was brutally murdered and then came back to life to save all the people that would accept who He truly is. Jesus did not try a quick fix. He made a lifelong commitment.

You must start making lifelong commitments to the vision God has given you about your health and all other aspects of life. If you have found yourself waiting for the moment you can eat anything and not have to exercise every day you are missing it. Ask God to renew your mind to accept that you must be intentional about how you eat and stay active. He will help you. God will bring you through every obstacle.

Keep thy heart with all diligence; for out of it are the issues of life.
Proverbs 4:23 KJV

For this light momentary affliction is preparing for us an eternal weight of glory beyond all comparison, as we look not to the things that are seen but to the things that are unseen. For the things that are seen are transient, but the things that are unseen are eternal. 2 Corinthians 4:17-18

Dear Lord,

I repent for having a quick fix mentality. I ask that you renew my mind so that I can be transformed and be a reflection of Christ and His Love for me. I surrender to the commitment of hard work and dedication just like Christ surrendered to death on the cross. I want to live a life pleasing to you Lord and I know my health matters. Help me understand why the way I think is so important. Help me keep my heart and have faith. In Jesus' name I pray. Amen.

Day Forty One

Don't Settle

When you set out to do a thing, you have most likely envisioned the end result. If you decided to cut your hair, after the stylist is finished you would not expect her to turn you toward the mirror and see yourself with more length to your hair than you began with. You would be disappointed and likely let her know that your hair should be shorter, not longer. You would probably demand a restyle or go to a different stylist who could make your hair look the way you envisioned it. You would not settle.

The goodness of the Lord is taking delight in Him, and Him giving you the desires of your heart.

The Lord wants you to have the desires of your heart. He wants you to experience abundant life. God is a God with all power and dominion and you are His child. Why would a God like that want you to settle when you don't have to settle? He doesn't!

People settle when they feel like the end result isn't worth fighting for any more. You should not be "fighting" for the things that matter most to you. You should be praying and

Being a BIG Deal

trusting God for these things to manifest, with faith that He will do it. The battle is not yours, it's the Lord's. God does not lose, so you should never settle.

I believe that I shall look upon the goodness of the Lord in the land of the living! Psalm 27:13

And let us not be not weary in well doing: for in due season you will reap, if you faint not. Galatians 6:9 KJV

Dear Lord,

I realize I cannot fight and win battles that do not belong to me. I turn all the worry and frustration over to you so that you can handle them for me. Lord I don't want to settle. I will not settle. I have faith that you will show me the end result of what I believe you for. Thank you for being all powerful in every circumstance. In Jesus' name I pray. Amen.

Day Forty Two

Begin Again

In life when one thing ends another thing begins. Often we think that once a goal has been met, we don't have to put in as much work anymore. An accomplished goal can be equated to a completed task. A task can be looked at as one piece to a big picture. There are many accomplishments and setbacks that form the makeup of who you are. Finishing a task--completing a goal--is only the beginning of who you are now. It is time for improvement and going to the next level. It is time to conquer the next goal of your dreams. Just because you have completed a goal does not mean the next goal will be easier, nor does it mean it will be harder. The next goal however, must be completed. With at least one goal completed that you have worked extremely hard to accomplish, you now possess the leverage of knowing you can do it. You now know you can push past the obstacles, the self-doubt, the outside voices, and anything trying to keep you away from your next achievements. You know that God is with you every step of the way. You know that God does not fail so, with God, you cannot fail. You are

Being a BIG Deal

empowered and you are successful. Congratulations on completing your forty-two day challenge and your new way of thinking. Congratulations on accomplishing every future God-given goal you set, because this end is just the beginning.

Blessed is the man who trusts in the Lord, whose trust is the Lord.
Jeremiah 17:7

I can do all things through Christ who strengthens me.
Philippians 4:13 NKJV

Dear Lord,

I am overjoyed that you have allowed me to see the manifestation of success. Thank you for leading me and guiding me through every step of the way. Even when I was afraid that I would fail, you kept me. Even when I was not perfect, you sustained me. Thank you for building my faith, my character, and my discernment for you through this process. I cannot thank you enough. I give you all the glory and I praise you Lord. In Jesus' name I pray. Amen.

Being a BIG Deal

"Always a Work in Progress"
(Top left November 2015, top right January 2016,
Bottom left February 2016, bottom right April 2016)

Literally made room for God to move!

Being a BIG Deal

Being a BIG Deal

Rob and me
(Left pic: May 2015, Right pic: May 2016)

My siblings and me after a workout
(Brooke and Christopher)

Being a BIG Deal

(Left to right Robin Brooks, Sarah Lindsey, & me)